preteen Bible study series

Handling Conflict

Loveland, Colorado

Group's R.E.A.L. Guarantee® to you:
This Group resource incorporates our R.E.A.L. approach to ministry—one that encourages long-term retention and life transformation. It's ministry that's:

Relational
Because learner-to-learner interaction enhances learning and builds Christian friendships.

Experiential
Because what learners experience through discussion and action sticks with them up to 9 times longer than what they simply hear or read.

Applicable
Because the aim of Christian education is to equip learners to be both hearers and doers of God's Word.

Learner-based
Because learners understand and retain more when the learning process takes into consideration how they learn best.

Handling Conflict

Copyright © 2004 Group Publishing, Inc.

All rights reserved. No part of this book may be reproduced in any manner whatsoever without prior written permission from the publisher, except where noted in the text and in the case of brief quotations embodied in critical articles and reviews. For information write Permissions, Group Publishing, Inc., Dept. PD, P.O. Box 481, Loveland, CO 80539.

Visit our Web site: www.grouppublishing.com

Credits
Author: Gary Wilde
Editors: Tammy L. Bicket and Dawn M. Brandon
Creative Development Editor: Karl Leuthauser
Chief Creative Officer: Joani Schultz
Copy Editor: Christy Fagerlin
Art Director: Kari K. Monson
Cover Art Director/Designer: Jeff Spencer
Cover Photographer: Daniel Treat
Print Production Artist: Tracy K. Hindman
Illustrator: Shawn Banner
Production Manager: DeAnne Lear

Unless otherwise noted, Scripture taken from the HOLY BIBLE, NEW INTERNATIONAL VERSION®. Copyright © 1973, 1978, 1984 by International Bible Society. Used by permission of Zondervan Publishing House. All rights reserved.

ISBN 0-7644-2494-7
10 9 8 7 6 5 4 3 2 1   13 12 11 10 09 08 07 06 05 04
Printed in the United States of America.

Contents

Introduction 5

Study 1: Being Christlike in Conflict 7
  The Point: We can be Christlike in conflict.
  Scripture Source: Genesis 4:2b-9; Ephesians 4:31-32

Study 2: Handling Conflict God's Way 19
  The Point: The best way to handle conflict with authorities is to speak the truth in love.
  Scripture Source: 1 Samuel 25:14-35; 26:7-21;
    2 Samuel 11:2-5, 14-15; 12:1-7a, 13; Ephesians 4:15, 25

Study 3: Reflecting Christ in Friendships 29
  The Point: We can learn to treat our friends fairly even in the midst of real conflict.
  Scripture Source: Matthew 18:21-35; Galatians 2:11-14

Study 4: Serving God at Home 39
  The Point: Giving and receiving trust is the key to getting along with parents.
  Scripture Source: 1 Samuel 20:24-34; Ephesians 6:1-4

Changed 4 Life 48

Introduction: Handling Conflict

Who doesn't have conflict? *Conflict* isn't a word just for the adult world. Every student in your class knows what it's like to face conflict daily. Some of these conflicts are ordinary, everyday ones—squabbles between siblings or friends about what belongs to whom or who gets to make decisions. Other conflicts are larger, more sinister. Many preteens are facing conflicts that could change or damage their lives. You might be surprised at what's going on in some of your kids' lives.

Whatever the magnitude, every conflict kids face is important, and they need to learn how to deal with conflict effectively and in ways that please God. This course will help students deal with conflict according to principles outlined in the Bible.

> When conflict results in constructive actions, it becomes a springboard for deeper communication, successful reconciliation, and a closer walk with Jesus.

In the first study, preteens will examine the concept of conflict. They'll learn that conflict isn't necessarily a bad thing—unless they allow it to generate and maintain a life of its own. Kids will understand that although they can't avoid all conflict, they can control how they respond to it, and they'll want to choose to respond in a Christlike manner.

In study two, kids will learn how to handle conflicts with those in authority over them by speaking the truth in love.

Next, preteens will learn and practice reflecting Christ's love as they resolve conflicts with friends. They'll learn rules for "fighting fair," confronting directly, and focusing on what friends have in common in the midst of their differences.

Finally, kids will examine conflict with parents. They'll see that serving God by giving and receiving trust is the key to maintaining good relationships with parents, and they'll strive to earn that respect while freely bestowing it on parents.

These studies will help kids learn to resolve conflicts in the way God would want them to. They can learn to discuss problems, negotiate solutions, and offer forgiveness and new starts. When conflict results in constructive actions like these, it becomes a springboard for deeper communication, successful reconciliation, and a closer walk with Jesus.

About Faith 4 Life™: Preteen Bible Study Series

The Faith 4 Life™: Preteen Bible Study Series helps preteens take a Bible-based approach to faith and life issues. Each book in the series contains these important elements:

- **Life application of Bible truth**—Faith 4 Life studies help preteens understand what the Bible says, and then apply that truth to their lives.

- **A relevant topic**—Each Faith 4 Life book focuses on one main topic, with four studies to give your students a thorough understanding of how the Bible relates to that topic.

- **One point**—Each study makes one point, centering on that one theme to make sure students really understand the important truth it conveys. This point is stated upfront and throughout the study.

- **Simplicity**—The studies are easy to use. Each contains a "Before the Study" box that outlines any advance preparation required. Each study also contains a "Study at a Glance" chart so you can quickly and easily see what supplies you'll need and what each study will involve.

- **Action and interaction**—Each study relies on experiential learning to help students learn what God's Word has to say. Preteens discuss and debrief their experiences in large groups, small groups, and individual reflection.

- **Reproducible handouts**—Faith 4 Life books include reproducible handouts for students. No need for student books!

- **Flexible options**—Faith 4 Life preteen studies have two opening and two closing activities. You can choose the options that work best for your students, time frame, or supply needs.

- **Follow-up ideas**—At the end of each book, you'll find a section called "Changed 4 Life." This provides ideas for following up with your students to make sure the Bible truths stick with them.

Use Faith 4 Life studies to show your preteens how the Bible is relevant to their lives. Help them see that God can invade every area of their lives and change them in ways they can only imagine. Encourage your students to go deeper into faith—faith that will sustain them for life! Faith 4 Life, forever!

Being Christlike in Conflict

The Point: ▶ We can be Christlike in conflict.

Conflict is neither right nor wrong, good nor bad. It's just a part of life that happens when people have different needs.

Yet our reactions to conflict *do* have a moral flavor. We can decide whether to work through our problems with others in a Christlike way or to devastate our opponents with whatever power we can muster. Help your preteens see that the options are many and the choices are theirs.

Scripture Source

Genesis 4:2b-9

In this passage, we read the story of Cain's frustration with God and jealousy of Abel's success.

Typically, conflict arises when a person tries to meet his or her needs at the expense of someone else. Cain wanted God's approval and equal status with Abel. But because of his disobedience to God, he was denied both. Cain's jealousy of Abel produced a conflict situation that could have been resolved in peaceful ways—through repentance, a change of attitude, and a new path of action. Instead, Cain chose the most extreme expression of "I win; you lose."

Growing kids experience loads of frustration and jealousy as they struggle to get the things they want on the path to adulthood. This Bible passage can remind them of the danger of putting their own needs ahead of others' at all costs.

Ephesians 4:31-32

In this passage, Paul tells believers to live lives that are radically different from their former lifestyles apart from Christ.

In the context of his teachings about putting on the "new self," Paul urges the Ephesians to get rid of all sinful expressions of anger that are incompatible with God's indwelling Spirit. Instead, we should follow Christ's example of forgiveness.

For preteens, part of the task of moving into adulthood is learning to control their reactions to hurt and injustice. For the Christian preteen, this means handling frustrations through the spirit-directed path of prayer and forgiveness. There may be times when it's appropriate to staunchly confront evil and stand up for what's right. Yet kids need to see that God is in control and that they can trust him with the outcome of every unjust or frustrating situation in their lives.

The Study at a Glance

Section	Minutes	What Students Will Do	Supplies
Warm-Up Option 1	up to 10	**Bean Bargain**—Try to win a prize in an unstructured game by getting the greatest number of beans.	Dried beans, prize, newsprint, marker, tape
Warm-Up Option 2	up to 10	**Bombs Away**—Write conflict situations on sheets of paper, then crumple the papers and bomb the other team.	Paper, pencils
Bible Connection	up to 20	**A Matter of Perspective**—Draw pictures of the same object using instructions with different perspectives, and recognize that conflict often results from people's different perspectives.	Bibles, lists of instructions, newsprint, markers, drawing paper, pencils or markers
	up to 15	**Happy-Ending Replay**—Use conflict-resolution strategies to replay the ending of the Cain and Abel story.	Bible, "Happy-Ending Replay" handout (p. 16), pencils, coins, newsprint, marker
Life Application	up to 15	**Reaction Roundup**—Identify with objects that represent conflict-resolution styles.	Bible, baseball bat, earmuffs, blanket, two-piece candy bar, ribbon, newsprint, marker, tape, pencils, "Conflict Control" handout (p. 17)
Wrap-Up Option 1	up to 5	**Standing Prayer**—Ask God's help for wise conflict resolution in the future.	
Wrap-Up Option 2	up to 5	**One More Time**—Discuss a recent conflict, telling their partners how it could've been handled.	

Before the Study

If you choose the "Bombs Away" warm-up option, set up chairs facing each other across the room. You may want to make a dividing line down the center of your room using masking tape.

For the "Matter of Perspective" activity, write each of the following lists on pieces of newsprint or poster board:

Team 1
It has four short legs.
Its back is arched.
It is brown.
It has spots.
It sits by the window.

Team 2
It has two arms.
It's four feet tall.
It's pleasingly plump.
It has a skirt.
It has buttons down the front.

For the "Happy-Ending Replay" activity, make a copy of the "Happy-Ending Replay" handout (p. 16) for each student.

For the "Reaction Roundup" activity, make a copy of the "Conflict Control" handout (p. 17) for each student. On a sheet of newsprint, list what conflict-resolution style each of the following objects represents: a baseball bat (physical violence); a pair of earmuffs (verbal abuse); a blanket (hidden anger, isolation); a two-piece candy bar (compromise, willingness to talk); and a piece of ribbon (the gift of forgiveness given to another person).

The Study

Warm-Up Option 1

Bean Bargain *(up to 10 minutes)*

Give kids each ten dried beans. Then display the prize you've brought—make it something kids like, such as a huge candy bar. The instructions you'll give for this game will be intentionally brief and vague.

Say: Here is the grand prize. Whoever has the most beans at the end of two minutes wins the prize. I'm going to leave it up to you to figure out how to get more beans from the others. Be inventive! You may want to trade something for more beans or negotiate in some other way. But let's remember to be respectful to one another in the process, or the game will end sooner, and you will be asked to forfeit your beans. OK? Ready! Set! Go!

Many of the kids will want more instruction. Others will start into the competition on their own terms. Just keep looking at your watch. The activity is deliberately open-ended to let kids experience how they deal with their conflicting needs to win and to know the rules and play fair.

It's likely some kids will aggressively confront others to get their beans; some will choose negotiation; others will withdraw. The situation is one of inherent conflict based on each person's need to have something that others are unwilling to give up.

> **FYI**
> *Keep a close eye to make sure the activity does not escalate. If you feel the activity is growing too aggressive, call time early, or ask the aggressive players to sit down and forfeit their beans.*

FYI

You may wish to further discuss the conflict-resolution styles that students displayed in the "Bean Bargain" activity. People who have studied conflict-resolution styles say there are five main ways people deal with conflict. Write the following list on a sheet of newsprint, and tape it to a wall:

1. Fight (I win; you lose.)
2. Avoid (I want out; I withdraw.)
3. Surrender (I give in to keep the peace.)
4. Compromise (I'll meet you halfway.)
5. Resolve (I'll go through it with you; we'll work on the problem together.)

Say: In this activity you saw people react to conflict in different ways. Take a moment to think about how you handled this conflict situation. **Ask:**

• What do you think your typical conflict-resolution style might be?

The Point ▶

When the two minutes are up, total each person's beans, and declare the winner. **Ask:**

• How hard was it to get what you needed, and how did that make you feel?

• Which of you tried to get beans by trading with other kids? by intimidating kids or working with others to gang up on somebody?

• How is dealing with conflict in this game like dealing with conflict in real life?

Say: Since we're looking at conflict in this session, it's important to realize from the start that conflict is a result of people trying to meet their own needs. ▶**We can be Christlike in conflict.** We all have natural ways of dealing with conflict, but what we do naturally isn't always the best thing. The Bible has some interesting things to teach us about conflict. Let's take a look.

Warm-Up Option 2

Bombs Away *(up to 10 minutes)*

Divide the group into two "nations." Have them sit in chairs on opposite sides of the room with an imaginary line separating them. Give each person a sheet of paper and a pencil.

Say: I want each of you to write one problem or conflict that might lead to war between two nations. Then, while remaining seated, crumple your paper into a "bomb." When I say, "Commence firing," you can throw your bomb at the other nation.

After the bombing, have kids each pick up one of the "enemy's" crumpled bombs, read what's on it, and tell how the problem could be resolved without violence. **Ask:**

• How did you feel when the other nation was bombing you?

• How did you feel when you fired your own bomb?

• How are these feelings like the way you feel when you're in the middle of a conflict with someone?

• Why do countries spend lives and money to go to war?

Say: One reaction to disagreements is to force your own way on others, even to the point of physical violence. ▶**We can be Christlike in conflict.** This course is about alternatives and choices we can make in conflict situations. I think you'll be surprised to discover how you can be like Jesus as you settle conflicts.

Bible Connection

A Matter of Perspective *(up to 20 minutes)*

Divide the class into two groups. Give each student a sheet of paper and access to colored pencils, pens, or crayons. Bring out the brief description lists you prepared before the study, and give one to each team. Instruct team members to draw a picture of something based on their list. If possible, have teams face away from each other so they won't see the other team's list.

Say: You have one minute to draw a picture based on the information on your list. It doesn't have to be a work of art. It just has to communicate what you think your object is. Ready! Set! Go!

Members of Team 1 will likely draw an animal. Members of Team 2 will probably draw a human being—most likely a young girl. After one minute, call time and remove the lists from view. Divide the class into pairs, with one student from each team in every pair. Before the partners get together and compare drawings, **say: Although your guidelines weren't exactly alike, both lists were describing the same object—so your pictures should all show the same object. Get together with your partner from the other team, and see how similar your drawings are. You have two minutes to show your picture to your partner and explain why you drew what you did. Then resolve the conflict so you both agree, and draw another picture.**

Chances are pairs will find it difficult to reconcile the two sets of instructions, but it will be interesting to see the variety of creative responses. After a few minutes, reveal that both lists were describing a chair. Go through both sets of instructions again with this in mind to see how seeing the big picture clarifies both sides' incomplete and faulty understanding and helps resolve conflict.

Ask:

• **Why was it so difficult for you and your partner to draw the same object based on the two different perceptions you had from your lists?**

• **Was one of you closer to being right than the other?**

• **What was the way to resolve the conflict, get at the truth, and draw a correct picture?**

• **How does this illustrate a major cause of conflicts we face with others?**

• **Would it make it easier for you to respond well to conflict to recognize that you might be seeing two different, incomplete facets of the same, greater truth? Why or why not?**

Ask a volunteer to read Genesis 4:2b-9 aloud while the other students follow along in their Bibles.

Ask:

• Cain and Abel approached God in very different ways and reached opposite conclusions. What was different about Cain's and Abel's sacrifices? about God's response to them? about their attitudes?

• What are some possible reasons Cain's sacrifice might not have been acceptable to God?

• From Genesis 4:7, what did God say to Cain that shows he could have chosen a response to conflict that was positive and pleasing to God?

• Cain lost track of the big picture and made a terrible mistake. What was the big picture that would have helped Cain choose to respond well? Was his original sacrifice meant to honor God or to show up his brother?

• Cain failed at both, but his poor response to conflict ensured an even greater failure in the end. What might have happened if Cain had followed God's urging to control or master his anger?

The Point ▶

Say: It's not always possible to avoid conflict. People have different perspectives, past experiences, and goals. ▶**We can be Christlike in conflict.** We can choose to please God by controlling ourselves and responding kindly and gently to those with whom we disagree.

Happy-Ending Replay *(up to 15 minutes)*

Say: Conflict is a natural part of life. We can't always choose to avoid it, but we can always choose how to respond to it. When we choose to let our reactions get out of control, it usually results in making the conflict worse and hurting everyone involved.

Ask:

• So how can we make good choices about how we'll respond to conflict?

Ask a student to read Ephesians 4:31-32 aloud. Hang up two pieces of newsprint. Draw a big minus symbol on one and a plus sign on the second. As students call out answers from the verses, write on the minus sheet those reactions and attitudes they must choose to lose in order to make the right choices in conflict. Write on the plus sheet those actions and attitudes they must choose to adopt.

Give kids an opportunity to apply these principles to the story of Cain and Abel.

Give kids each a photocopy of the "Happy-Ending Replay" handout (p. 16), a pencil, and a Bible. Form pairs and have each pair flip a coin to determine who will take the role of Cain and who will be Abel. Give the pairs a few minutes to work through the handout.

Then bring the group together. Ask kids to share their problem-solving ideas for Cain and Abel. Then **ask:**

- **What needs did Cain have that resulted in his action against Abel?**
- **What did Cain do wrong according to Ephesians 4:31-32?**
- **What could he have done better?**
- **What do you think kept Cain from choosing to respond well to his conflict with Abel? How easy is it to choose a good, God-honoring response in the midst of conflict?**

Form pairs. Have one person in each pair be the speaker and the other be the listener. Have speakers tell their partners about a time they had a "happy ending" to a conflict. Have listeners then say how their partner did a good job handling the conflict.

For example, the speaker might say, "My sister and I always argued about her wearing my clothes. Now we work it out by deciding at the beginning of the week which clothes we'll share instead of fighting at the last minute." The listener might then respond by saying, "You showed a loving attitude by being willing to share with your sister."

After a minute or two, have listeners and speakers switch roles and repeat the activity.

Say: Conflict resolution takes place when people on both sides decide to look at the problem objectively and work through it together. It may mean giving something up, but you'll get a happy ending and a stronger relationship in return.

Life Application

Reaction Roundup *(up to 15 minutes)*

Set up five objects on an imaginary line that goes from one end of the room to another. As you lay out the items, explain what they represent: a baseball bat (physical violence); a pair of earmuffs (verbal abuse); a blanket (hidden anger, isolation); a two-piece candy bar (compromise, willingness to talk); and a piece of ribbon (the gift of forgiveness given to another person). Then post on the wall the list of these items and their meanings that you prepared before the study so students can use it as a reference.

The Point ▶

Read Ephesians 4:31-32 aloud once again to set the standard for conflict resolution. **Say:** ▶**We can be Christlike in conflict. We can choose a God-honoring way to resolve conflict rather than just reacting. The problem is, we usually react—in the negative ways these verses point out—instead of making the choice for solving the conflict.**

Explain that you're going to describe different conflict situations. After each one, kids should stand next to the object that shows how they think they'd most likely react. Encourage kids to be honest.

Here are the situations:

1. You get stuck mowing the lawn at home instead of going out with friends.

2. You want to change the channel, but your brother says no and continues watching cartoons.

3. A classmate accuses you of cheating on a test, but she was the one who cheated off you.

4. You and your friend are standing outside a movie theater, and you each want to see different shows.

5. You're late getting home, and your dad yells that you're irresponsible.

6. You walk in a park, and a man pushes you down and steals your wallet or purse.

Give kids each a photocopy of the "Conflict Control" handout (p. 17) and a pencil. Give them a moment to fill in the "Conflict-Predictor" box.

Say: Move to the object that symbolizes how you want to respond, with God's help, to the conflict you predicted. Then read through the "Ground Rules." After each one, close your eyes, and imagine yourself taking that step. After you've worked through the whole process, write your own happy ending to the conflict situation you predicted.

Wrap-Up Option 1

Standing Prayer *(up to 5 minutes)*

Have kids sit near the object representing how they'd like to respond to the conflict they predicted they'd be facing. Ask students to bow their heads and pray a simple prayer, asking God to see where they're standing and asking him to help them stand in the same place when conflict hits.

Wrap-Up Option 2

One More Time *(up to 5 minutes)*

Have kids pair up again with their partners from the "Happy-Ending Replay" activity. Have them each tell of a recent conflict in their lives and how they handled it. Then have partners brainstorm other options for handling the conflict based on what they've learned in today's study. Close with a moment for partners to pray silently for each other to handle conflict gracefully.

Extra-Time Tips

Use these extra ideas to add some creative fun to your studies. They are low-prep or no-prep ideas that work in no time!

Work It Out—Form groups of no more than four. Have each group pick one of the conflict situations from the "Reaction Roundup" activity. Have groups plan and perform role-plays showing both positive and negative solutions to their conflict.

In My Opinion—Write on a chalkboard or newsprint: "Conflict is a natural part of life."

Then **ask:**

- **Do you agree or disagree with this statement? Explain.**
- **What would you add to this statement to make it clearer or more complete?**

Happy-Ending ◀ REPLAY

Read through the story in Genesis 4:2b-9 with your partner. Then flip a coin to choose roles—heads for Cain, tails for Abel. Work through these problem-solving steps to reach a happier ending to the story. Write how you'll deal with each step in the space below.

	Cain	**Abel**

1. Describe the problem.
Go to the other person and agree to look at the problem. No blaming!

2. Brainstorm solutions.
How could the problem be solved? No ideas are too weird.

3. Find areas of agreement.
List the solutions that appeal to both people.

4. Develop a course of action.
What steps can you take to resolve the conflict, based on the areas of agreement?

Permission to photocopy this handout from Faith 4 Life™: Preteen Bible Study Series, *Handling Conflict* granted for local church use. Copyright © Group Publishing, Inc., P.O. Box 481, Loveland, CO 80539. www.grouppublishing.com

Conflict-Predictor

One conflict I know I'll face in the near future is…

Ground Rules

Use these ground rules to help you reach a solution.

1. Accept conflict as a natural part of life.

2. Remember to attack the problem, not the person.

3. Talk about your own feelings. Say, "I feel…" instead of, "You are…"

4. Be committed to giving more than you take.

5. Listen! Try to feel the other person's feelings.

6. Avoid tactics designed only to get what you want.

7. Be willing to admit mistakes. Be the first to say, "I'm sorry."

8. Be ready to offer forgiveness, just as Christ has forgiven you.

My Happy Ending

Handling Conflict God's Way

The Point: ▶ The best way to handle conflict with authorities is to speak the truth in love.

During adolescence, kids gradually pull away from the authorities of their childhood. The challenge for kids is to learn how to express their needs—even the need to make a mistake—and still maintain respect for the authority figures in their lives.

Kids must realize that not even adults are completely free from authority. From the local police officer to the Internal Revenue Service to God, some form of authority is always with us, and that can be tough to handle.

From today's study, preteens can learn that the best approach to conflict with authority is direct and honest speech that conveys feelings as well as needs. With this kind of communication, either side—usually both—can grasp the opportunity to repent and change for the better.

Scripture Source

1 Samuel 25:14-35

This passage recounts Abigail's wise intervention when an angry David sought vengeance against her husband and household. Abigail's example of gentle words, compliments, wisdom, and appealing to David's better nature are important for preteens to emulate when in conflict with authority figures.

1 Samuel 26:7-21

This passage shows how David spoke the truth to King Saul to defend himself against Saul's unfair accusations. That David could confront Saul's error without fighting back, trying to hurt him, or taking vengeance is an important example for preteens.

2 Samuel 11:2-5, 14-15; 12:1-7a, 13

Second Samuel 11 sets the stage for King David's sin with Bathsheba and murder of her husband. Second Samuel 12 shows Nathan confronting King David. By telling a story that moves David to clear thinking and repentance, Nathan illustrates the courage, wisdom, and love that's needed to successfully resolve conflicts with authority figures.

Ephesians 4:15, 25

The Apostle Paul calls for speaking the truth in love. Direct, honest speech helps us avoid dissension and is a characteristic of those who seek to live in the light.

The Study at a Glance

Section	Minutes	What Students Will Do	Supplies
Warm-Up Option 1	up to 10	**Fender Bender**—Imitate traffic accidents and the confrontations that follow.	Whistle, newsprint, marker, tape
Warm-Up Option 2	up to 10	**Sticky Snacks**—See how a drink cuts through sticky peanut butter (but how much more appealing is a cold, refreshing drink than a warm one), and compare this with tempering the truth with love.	Peanut butter, crackers, warm and ice-cold drinks
Bible Connection	up to 15	**Coached for Conflict**—Teams summarize biblical strategies for dealing with conflict and outline a playbook for speaking the truth in love.	Bibles, newsprint and markers or chalkboard and chalk
	up to 15	**Speak the Truth**—Write advice about speaking the truth, and then role-play using that advice.	Bibles, pencils, "Speak the Truth in Love" handout (p. 27)
Life Application	up to 15	**What's Your Track Record?**—Record personal experience in authority conflicts and give a blessing to a partner.	Pencils, "What's Your Track Record?" handout (p. 28)
Wrap-Up Option 1	up to 5	**Conflict Monsters**—Draw monsters to represent scary conflicts.	Newsprint, markers
Wrap-Up Option 2	up to 5	**Rap It Up**—Write a rap based on Scripture.	Bible, newsprint, markers

Before the Study

If you choose the "Sticky Snacks" option, prepare two sets of the same drink (water, soft drinks, or milk) for students. Be sure one set of drinks is room temperature while the other is ice-cold. One sure way to do this is to pack drink bottles in a cooler or tub with lots of ice. That makes drinks even cooler and more refreshing than when they're refrigerated.

For the "Coached for Conflict" activity, write the following questions on the chalkboard or on a piece of newsprint:

In this passage…

• Who was the authority figure?

• Who confronted the authority figure with truth that was difficult to say and hear?

- What part does courage play in conflicts with authority?
- What part do tact, respect, and love play?
- What was the plain truth about what the authority figure had done (or was about to do) wrong?
- How did the person truthfully confront the authority with what he or she believed was wrong?
- How did they soften the unpleasant truth with kindness, respect, and love?
- What difference did that make?
- What strategy can you learn from this person about how to speak truthfully to authority figures with whom you have conflict?

For the "What's Your Track Record?" activity, make a copy of the "What's Your Track Record?" handout (p. 28) for each student.

If you choose the "Rap It Up" activity, write the words of Proverbs 12:16 on a large sheet of newsprint: "A fool shows his annoyance at once, but a prudent man overlooks an insult."

The Study

Warm-Up Option 1

Fender Bender *(up to 10 minutes)*

Choose a volunteer to be a police officer. The rest of the kids will be vehicles. Have them circulate around with their elbows tucked into their sides and their forearms extended as if holding a steering wheel, making noises like cars and trucks. All their movements should be stiff and mechanical.

Say: The vehicles must move around the room at random until I blow the whistle. Then they must stop immediately and follow my instructions to stop, turn left, speed up, make a U-turn, spin out, or whatever. Just as adults who drive must be careful to avoid hitting others, let's be careful so no one gets hurt.

The kids' task is to avoid touching other vehicles. If they do touch, the colliding parties must each yell, "Ouch!" Everybody then stops while the police officer listens to each collision victim's argument about who was at fault.

Instruct kids to argue in a manner that would show how real drivers are likely to handle the conflict when they get out of their cars and confront one another after a fender bender. Based on both drivers' stories and how they collided, the police officer should decide who is at fault in the accident.

The person at fault is taken to jail (out of the game). Play a few rounds to determine who the safest drivers are. Then gather the group together for discussion. **Ask:**

- **How did it feel to talk to the police officer about your accident?**
- **Did you think the police officer's decision was fair?**
- **Have you ever witnessed a discussion between someone and a police officer in real life? How did the participants behave?**
- **Why is it difficult to handle conflicts with people who are in authority over us?**
- **How difficult was it to be the police officer and to be responsible for making good decisions that are fair to everyone?**
- **Sometimes it's impossible for authorities to make decisions that please or seem fair to everyone. How does knowing this make it easier to sympathize with people in authority when we have conflicts with them?**

Ask kids to name some of the authorities to whom they have to answer. Write their responses on a sheet of newsprint taped to the wall.

Say: Sometimes you probably think having to answer to all these people is really the pits. But the picture doesn't change all that much when you become an adult. Handling conflicts with authorities is a tricky thing, but there are ways to do it effectively. We're going to look at some of these ways today.

The Point ▶ We'll learn that ▶**the best way to handle conflict with authorities is to speak the truth in love.**

Warm-Up Option 2

Sticky Snacks *(up to 10 minutes)*

Give students a dry, sticky snack of crackers loaded with peanut butter. Be sure each student gets several peanut butter crackers, as the goal is to get the snack stuck to the roof of his or her mouth and create a great need for a drink.

Say: This snack is a little like conflict with authority. Such conflict always involves two parts—us and the person in authority—like peanut butter and crackers. When we have conflict with those in authority over us, it creates a sticky situation that can be difficult to resolve.

Ask: What are some sticky conflicts you've had or that you've seen others have with authority figures?

Provide two drink options for students: one lukewarm and the other ice-cold and refreshing. You may choose to use warm and cold soft drinks, water, milk, or fruit drinks—as long as both options are the same. Just be sure that one option is tepid and unappealing while keeping the other stored in ice so it's really cold.

Urge students to sample both options, then choose the one they prefer to drink.

Ask:

• **Which drink do you prefer? Why?**

Say: **When we find ourselves in a sticky conflict with those in authority, nothing cuts through the conflict like speaking the truth. Speaking the truth is like this lukewarm water** [or other drink]. **It cuts through the peanut butter well enough, but it's not very appealing. Ephesians 4:15 teaches the importance of speaking the truth in love. When we speak the truth in love, it makes the truth much more attractive and easy for others to swallow. It's like the water** [or other drink] **on ice. Not only does it cut through the peanut butter and quench our thirst, but it's inviting and refreshing. Today we'll learn the importance of** ➤**handling conflict with authorities by speaking the truth in love.**

◀ *The Point*

Bible Connection

Coached for Conflict *(up to 15 minutes)*

Divide the class into three teams. Assign each team one of the following Bible passages: Abigail and David—1 Samuel 25:14-35, David and Saul—1 Samuel 26:7-21, and Nathan and David—2 Samuel 11:2-5, 14-15; 12:1-7a, 13. The goal of the entire class is to come up with a playbook for handling conflict with authority figures well. Each team is responsible for developing strategies based on their Bible passage, naming plays kids can use themselves ("the compliment cooldown" or "the long-distance 'listen-to-me'"), and then coaching the rest of the class on how to use these strategies for speaking the truth in love.

Have teams consider the following questions (that you wrote out before the study) when making their playbook for resolving conflicts with authorities:

Ask: **In this passage…**

• **Who was the authority figure?**

• **Who confronted the authority figure with plain truth that was difficult to say and hear?**

• **How did he or she soften the unpleasant truth with kindness, respect, and love, and what difference did that make?**

FYI

You may want to name the teams after popular local athletic teams or after national teams in a sport that's in season. Add to the athletic team/locker room atmosphere during this activity by wearing a baseball cap and sweats (or an athletic jacket) and sporting a whistle and clipboard.

• What strategy can you learn from this person about how to speak truthfully—with courage, tact, respect, and love—to authority figures with whom you may have conflict?

After students have worked for five to seven minutes, ask each team to present the plays they diagrammed (on newsprint or the chalkboard) for confronting conflict with authorities by speaking the truth in love. Help them recognize that

The Point ▶ ▶the best way to handle conflict with authorities is to speak the truth in love.

Speak the Truth *(up to 15 minutes)*

Say: **One of the main ways we can prevent conflicts—and deal with them when they occur—is to practice being direct and truthful in our speech patterns. Let's look at what Paul has to say about doing this.**

Give kids each a photocopy of the "Speak the Truth in Love" handout (p. 27) and a pencil. Read Ephesians 4:15, 25 aloud. Give kids about five minutes to write their advice. Then have kids tell what they wrote for each situation. **Ask:**

• **What's the hardest thing about speaking the truth in love?**

• **In what specific ways do you think speaking the truth could help you in conflicts with authority?**

Say: **Like any other skill, speaking the truth in love is something that needs to be learned and then practiced. It can make a difference in your life!**

Life Application

What's Your Track Record? *(up to 15 minutes)*

Give kids each a photocopy of the "What's Your Track Record?" handout (p. 28) and a pencil. Have them work through the handout with a partner.

The Point ▶ **Say:** **This handout will help you look at how you might handle conflicts with authority. Remember,** ▶**the best way to handle conflict with authorities is to speak the truth in love.**

Mark your responses, and discuss them with your partner. After your discussion, encourage your partner by filling in the blessing portion of the handout and giving it to him or her to keep during the rest of this course.

After a few minutes, form a circle, and have volunteers tell what they learned from the handout.

Wrap-Up Option 1

Conflict Monsters (up to 5 minutes)

Give kids each a sheet of newsprint and a marker. Ask them to think of a scary confrontation they've faced in the past, are facing now, or could imagine facing in the future. Tell them to picture this situation as a monster and draw that monster on their newsprint. As they're drawing, ask them to think about how Jesus would want them to confront their monsters.

Close the study by stacking the monsters and standing in a circle around them. Have kids join hands and pray silently for the strength to speak the truth in love in each of those conflict situations.

Then pray aloud for Jesus to give students strength. Have kids each tear their monsters in half, acknowledging Jesus' power over all the conflict situations in their lives.

Wrap-Up Option 2

Rap It Up (up to 5 minutes)

Post the words of Proverbs 12:16 that you wrote on the newsprint before the study: "A fool shows his annoyance at once, but a prudent man overlooks an insult."

Work as a group to paraphrase this verse into a rap song. For example, "You know you're a fool/when you blow your cool,/but a wise man/shuts his eyes, man."

Say: Sometimes it's best to let go of minor hurts and snubs in life rather than attacking people who have wronged you and creating a full-blown conflict. Have kids silently resolve to speak the truth in love. Then close with prayer.

Extra-Time Tips

Use these extra ideas to add some creative fun to your studies. They are low-prep or no-prep ideas that work in no time!

Professional Rappers—If you chose the "Rap It Up" closing, have kids work on expanding it and adding choreography. Then videotape the performance.

Prayers for Authority—Have each student "stand in" for someone in authority in their lives. You may want to give kids name tags bearing specific names (Pastor

Bob) or positions (teachers, parents, police). Then have groups of kids gather around each individual and pray for those leaders.

My Country: Right or Wrong?—Romans 13:1-7 gives instructions to Christians about how to relate to government authority. Coordinate an impromptu debate revolving around a specific current event. Ask kids to consider the Christian citizen's role in obeying or confronting the government's positions on this issue.

Speak the Truth in Love

Read Ephesians 4:15, 25. Then write your advice for each situation below.

1. Say a simple yes or no. Jesus tells us to do this in Matthew 5:37. When we "hem and haw" about things, we make it hard for people to figure out what we mean and what we really want.

Situation: Joe's youth minister asked him to be the youth group treasurer. Joe knew he was too busy to do it, but he said, "Well, I guess I could." The youth minister delivered the financial records to Joe and then angrily confronted him two months later when Joe had failed to show up at any youth meetings.

Advice: What advice would you give to a person who finds it hard to say no?

_____
_____

2. Use the ABC confrontation formula. The formula: "When you do A in situation B, I feel C. I want…" This is a non-threatening way to make a complaint or confront someone about his or her behavior. You tell your own feelings instead of blaming the other person.

Situation: John blurted out to his teacher, "You drive me crazy. You never listen to me. Why should I even try in this class? You always give me about two seconds to answer, and then you call on somebody else. Why don't you ever give me a chance?"

Advice: How could John have used the ABC confrontation formula to better express his feelings and needs?

_____
_____

3. Say, "I'm sorry," when you're wrong. It makes a big difference in settling conflicts if we're quick to admit when we're wrong. Repenting is a key to Christian living. It opens the door for deeper conversation and frees others to repent and receive forgiveness too.

Situation: When Mrs. Wilson accused Jane of cheating on her quiz, Jane glared and said, "Prove it!" Mrs. Wilson finally gave in and let Jane take the quiz again, but Jane decided just to stop talking to her for the rest of the semester.

Advice: What advice would you give Jane?

_____
_____
_____

 Permission to photocopy this handout from Faith 4 Life™: Preteen Bible Study Series, *Handling Conflict* granted for local church use. Copyright © Group Publishing, Inc., P.O. Box 481, Loveland, CO 80539. www.grouppublishing.com

What's Your Track Record?

Mark the answer that best describes how you might respond.

When I run into trouble with people in authority, I usually…

❏ pull away to avoid confrontation and responsibility.
❏ hold back my real feelings and try to be nice.
❏ try to blow them away with my anger.
❏ other (explain):

The way things usually turn out when I use this approach is…

❏ somebody gets run over.
❏ I come in last place.
❏ several contestants develop strained muscles.
❏ other (explain):

The main thing I need to do to improve my skill in conflict situations is…

❏ learn to head straight for the goal (use direct speech; say yes or no).
❏ practice better techniques (use the ABC confrontation formula).
❏ make faster turns (be ready to say I'm sorry when I'm wrong).
❏ other (explain):

Fill out this blessing, and give it to your partner.

_____, you are a valuable person who deserves to be heard and treated with respect. May God
       name
be with you as you seek to speak the truth in love in all conflict situations. I will say a prayer for you this week.

Signed _____

Date _____

Reflecting Christ in Friendships

The Point: ➤ We can learn to treat our friends fairly even in the midst of real conflict.

Many preteens are competitive by nature. Sometimes they have the mistaken impression that competing means trying to totally demolish the opposition. They tend to lose sight of what they're really competing for and turn on their competitors. So even friends can resort to unfriendly methods of verbal combat when a healthy competition turns unhealthy.

Just as there are rules for the various forms of competition, there are fair and unfair ways to handle interpersonal conflict. Encourage your students to choose the path of fairness, which results in mercy and forgiveness.

Scripture Source

Matthew 18:21-35

In this passage, Jesus responds to Peter's question about how many times to forgive someone by telling the parable of the unmerciful servant. Jesus' parable shows, ultimately, that Christian relationships are to be built on the foundation of mutual forgiveness and mercy.

Help preteens recognize that their relationships with friends can be based on their experience of God's unconditional love for them. Sometimes friends can be irritating, even downright aggravating. Yet we're called to love them with a portion of the divine love that's been poured into our own lives.

Galatians 2:11-14

In this passage, we read of a conflict between Paul and Peter regarding Peter's reverting to the old dietary laws when around certain Jewish legalists.

Paul's great theme in Galatians is that we're justified by faith alone, not by keeping the laws of the old covenant. Peter had apparently accepted that message wholeheartedly and was content to eat pork with Gentile converts. But when some people came from Jerusalem, he withdrew from his Gentile friends and traded his pork for lamb. Peter fell back into dietary restrictions that were still dear to those

Jewish Christians. This made Paul angry because it was a counterexample to his preaching themes.

This passage helps kids remember that conflict situations are rarely cut-and-dried instances of one person clearly being in the wrong and the other in the right. Both parties usually struggle with intense feelings and questions about just what is right and wrong.

The Study at a Glance

Section	Minutes	What Students Will Do	Supplies
Warm-Up Option 1	up to 10	**Escalating Compliments**—Pairs compete to give greater and greater compliments.	
Warm-Up Option 2	up to 10	**Destination: Chaos**—Try to arrive at different goals while tied together with yarn.	Poster board, markers, index cards, tape, yarn
Bible Connection	up to 20	**Baa, Baa, Oink, Oink**—Re-enact Paul's conflict with Peter, and practice conflict resolution.	Bible
	up to 15	**Fighting Fair**—Attempt to match cards describing unfair fighting methods.	"Unfair Fighting" handout (p. 38), scissors
Life Application	up to 10	**Tough to Say**—Silent partners try to say, "I'm sorry," with lips taped shut.	Transparent tape
Wrap-Up Option 1	up to 10	**Debtor Notes**—Write notes of appreciation to ease a conflict.	Bible, stamped postcards, pens
Wrap-Up Option 2	up to 10	**Love Feast**—Share bread and feelings with classmates.	Loaf of bread

Before the Study

If you choose the "Destination: Chaos" warm-up option, make four poster board signs, one with each of the following words: *ball game*, *movie*, *concert*, and *party*. Write one word on alternating index cards in sufficient quantities for each student to receive one index "destination" card.

For the "Fighting Fair" activity, make a copy of the "Unfair Fighting" handout (p. 38) for each team, and separate them into cards as indicated.

The Study

Warm-Up Option 1

Escalating Compliments *(up to 10 minutes)*

Form groups of four. Call one group to the front, and have kids in that group stand facing each other across a table, two on one side and two on the other.

Say: This is a compliment competition. Kids on each side of the table will take turns giving compliments to the other two. You'll start with ordinary compliments, but then try to make each compliment you give better than the one you just got. At the end of one minute, I'll stop you, and the rest of the class will vote on which pair gave the most wildly wonderful compliments.

Call time after one minute. Have the rest of the class score the pairs on a scale of one to ten (one is poor; ten is great), based on how well they showed an increase of emotion as they became more wildly profuse in their compliments. If you have time, give other groups a chance to compete in this activity.

Then **say: This exercise shows how "verbal jousting" can escalate among friends. It was fun to think of new compliments to shower on one another. But we all know that just the opposite happens when we get into fights—our emotions heat up, and our tongues can unleash some pretty nasty comments. How can we ▶learn to treat our friends fairly even in the midst of real conflict? That's what this session is all about.** ◀ *The Point*

Warm-Up Option 2

Destination: Chaos *(up to 10 minutes)*

Tape one of the four poster board signs you made before the study (with the words *ball game*, *movie*, *concert*, and *party*) to each wall of the room. Tie teams of three to six kids together at the ankles with a piece of yarn. Give kids each a "destination" index card with one of the four words written on it. Explain that kids are to keep their destinations a secret from the other members of their teams. Set up a natural conflict situation by giving at least two different destinations to kids on the same team.

Say: Your goal is to get to the destination that's written on your card. You may not talk to anyone or show anyone your card. You may only communicate

FYI

Make sure each student is wearing socks or pants under the yarn to avoid irritating the skin. Have extra socks on hand for kids who might need them.

with gestures. You have two minutes to arrive at your destination. If any team breaks its yarn, they're disqualified. OK, go!

Chaos is likely to break out as kids try to pull their teammates in different directions. Congratulate any team that actually manages to arrive at a destination. Find out who held the cards for that destination, and shake their hands. Then call the teams together for discussion. **Ask:**

• **How did you feel, trying to get the other kids on your team to move in the direction you wanted to go?**

• **What methods did you use to try to influence your team to move in a particular direction?**

• **How was this activity like real-life conflicts between friends?**

• **What methods do you normally use to influence your friends' decisions?**

• **What kinds of issues can cause fighting among friends?**

The Point ▶

• **How can we learn to ▶treat our friends fairly even in the midst of real conflict?**

Say: Conflicts among friends are bound to happen simply because people have different needs and goals. The important thing to remember is that there's a right way to fight and a wrong way. Handling conflicts the right way can build stronger relationships. Handling conflicts the wrong way can mean the end of a friendship.

The Point ▶

That's what this session is all about. ▶We can learn to treat our friends fairly even in the midst of real conflict. Let's find out how.

FYI

It's OK to have girls play the parts of male Bible characters. If you don't, you'll effectively deny girls key avenues of involvement. Try to involve every student regularly, but strive to keep both genders represented fairly and positively.

Bible Connection

Baa, Baa, Oink, Oink *(up to 20 minutes)*

Select three students—one to represent Peter, one to represent Paul, and one to represent Barnabas. Divide the rest of the class into two groups—one (the Baas) to represent the Jews and one (the Oinks) to represent the non-Jews (Gentiles).

Explain that for many centuries, Jews had been God's special people with a covenant that demanded obedience to God through a complex series of rules and dietary laws. But after Jesus Christ died on the cross and was raised from the dead, believing in him became the only way to salvation. Faith in Jesus made one a Christian, not the old rules and dietary laws. So when people who had never been

Jews started becoming Christians, they didn't follow the Jewish laws. They had different cultural rules and traditions.

But a lot of Jewish Christians had trouble with the changes. They had a hard time distinguishing between what was really the core of being part of the family of Christ and what was a matter of preference or culture. That could cause many hurt feelings and problems, as students will see today. That's the basis of the conflict between Peter and Paul, two friends who worked together and had the same goals—to share God's truth with everyone.

Say: One of the Jews' dietary laws said that it was wrong to eat pork, so Jews in Paul's day ate a lot of lamb. That's why those of you who are representing the Jews in this story will speak with lambs' voices. For the next few minutes, you can't use any real words. You can only baa like a sheep.

But the Gentiles had no such rules. They ate a lot of pork. That's why those of you who are representing the Gentiles in this story will speak with pigs' voices. For the next few minutes, you can't use any real words. You can only oink like pigs. Both groups must use tone, expressions, and body language to communicate. Consider how the character you represent must have been feeling at each point in this conflict, and try to communicate that.

Have a volunteer read Galatians 2:11-14 aloud slowly, pausing between verses so you can guide the other kids to act out the story following these instructions:

Verse 11: "When Peter came to Antioch, I opposed him to his face, because he was clearly in the wrong." Paul should be confronting Peter with a series of oinks and baas.

Verse 12: "Before certain men came from James, he used to eat with the Gentiles." Peter should re-enact eating and enjoying fellowship with the Gentiles using only oinks.

"But when they arrived, he began to draw back and separate himself from the Gentiles because he was afraid of those who belonged to the circumcision group." Then the Baas should come along, baaing loudly and disapprovingly at Peter, who eventually puts away his pig's tail, moves away from the Oinks, and starts speaking only in baas.

Verse 13: "The other Jews joined him in his hypocrisy, so that by their hypocrisy even Barnabas was led astray." Barnabas follows Peter's example. The Oinks might respond with hurt or indignant oinks. The Baas might look and sound superior and self-satisfied. Peter and Barnabas may feel guilty or uncomfortable.

To add to the fun, consider giving group members white cotton balls to fluff into sheep's ears or pink chenille craft wires to twist into curly pigs' tails to further help identify the distinct groups. Give students representing Peter, Paul, and Barnabas one of each to show that they could get along in either group. Also give each student a cross made simply of paper, straws, or craft sticks. Help kids recognize that people usually have a choice. They can focus on what makes people different, or they can find the common ground and focus on what friends share and how they are alike. One way increases conflict; the second way resolves it.

Verse 14: "When I saw that they were not acting in line with the truth of the gospel, I said to Peter in front of them all, 'You are a Jew, yet you live like a Gentile and not like a Jew. How is it, then, that you force Gentiles to follow Jewish customs?' " Paul is again confronting Peter in a series of oinks and baas. The students playing Peter and Barnabas must decide how to react. What will they do?

Say: That was a silly way of representing a serious conflict. Now you can speak English again. Talk through the situation to practice your conflict-resolution skills on something that isn't so personal and emotional to you. **How will you resolve the conflict?**

Allow five minutes for kids to try to talk through possible solutions to the conflict. Then **ask:**

- **How did you resolve this conflict?**
- **Why do you think Peter gave in to pressure in the first place?**
- **How did the Baas make you Oinks feel? Was it worse when Peter followed their lead and abandoned you?**
- **Why was it so important for Paul to confront this problem head on and in public? What does the fact that other Jews and Barnabas followed Peter's bad example have to do with it?**
- **What might have happened to the Gentiles' new faith in Christ if they had continued to be rejected and condemned by Jewish Christians?**
- **How was that contrary to what Paul and Peter were both working for?**

The Point ▶ **Say:** ▶**We can learn to treat our friends fairly even in the midst of real conflict.** It was important for Paul to address his disagreement with Peter quickly so it could be corrected. Too often we let slights or disagreements fester without saying anything. That just makes them grow bigger. It's like a little pebble in your shoe or something stuck in your teeth that eventually consumes all your attention. We need to make an overall commitment to fighting fair. Let's see just what that means.

Fighting Fair *(up to 15 minutes)*

Form teams of six. Each team will need one photocopy of the "Unfair Fighting" handout (p. 38), cut up into cards. Give team members each one Foul Card and one Loose-Lips Card.

Say: The object of this game is to match your Foul Cards with the correct Loose-Lips Cards. The person with Foul Card 1 will read it aloud. If you think you have the Loose-Lips Card that demonstrates that unfair fighting technique, slap the card down on the table (or floor). Then read it aloud. See if your teammates agree that you have the matching card. If you think you have a match, place the cards side by side on the table (or floor). Then go on to Foul Card 2. The first team to correctly match all its cards wins.

The correct matches are 1—B; 2—E; 3—C; 4—A; 5—D; 6—F.

After the game, **say:** ►**We can learn to treat our friends fairly even in the midst of real conflict.** Learning how to have a "fair fight" may be one of the most important skills you'll gain in this class.

Have kids re-examine Galatians 2:11-14 as they discuss these questions. **Ask:**

• **What examples of fair fighting can you find in Paul's description of this incident?**

• **Do you think Paul was setting a bad example by allowing this conflict between two prominent church leaders to be seen? Why or why not?**

• **Why is it especially important for Christians to fight fair?**

Say: If we remember to avoid what's on these Foul Cards, we'll go a long way toward learning to handle conflicts with our friends in the right way. But there's also another important thing we need to learn to do.

Life Application

Tough to Say *(up to 10 minutes)*

Form pairs. Give one partner in each pair a four-inch length of transparent tape.

Say: Each of you holding the tape, please use it to tape your partner's mouth shut. When you "silent partners" have been taped, come over to me for your instructions.

Make a huddle with the kids whose mouths have been taped. Explain in a whisper that they are to say the words *I'm sorry* to their partners. They can try as many times as they want, but they can't take the tape off their lips. When kids are ready, give the word for the silent partners to say, "I'm sorry."

After the silent partners have had a few tries, ask if anyone knows what his or her partner was trying to say. Then let the silent partners remove their pieces of tape. **Ask:**

FYI

If you have fewer than six students in your class or on any one team, it's OK to give more than one Foul Card and more than one Loose-Lips Card to each one.

◄ *The Point*

- How did you feel when you tried to say, "I'm sorry," with your mouth taped?
- How is that like the way people feel when they have to say, "I'm sorry," after making a mistake or hurting a friend?
- Why is it so hard to say, "I'm sorry"?

Say: In the heat of conflict, it's really tough to be the first to say, "I'm sorry"—or at least offer some form of truce. It means making a decision to let down our defenses in order to start healing the relationship. It's not easy, but somebody has to do it.

Give kids each a small piece of transparent tape. Have them each stick it on the inside of their forearm (under their clothing).

The Point ▶

Say: ▶We can learn to treat our friends fairly even in the midst of real conflict. One way to do that is to be willing and quick to say you're sorry, even when the other person won't—even when you feel like it's more his or her fault than yours. Perhaps your lips have been sealed when you could have said, "I'm sorry." Wear this tape for the rest of the day. Each time you notice it, ask God to help you be willing to say, "I'm sorry," when you find yourself in future conflicts. Look for opportunities this week to say you're sorry.

Wrap-Up Option 1

Debtor Notes *(up to 10 minutes)*

Call on a volunteer to read Matthew 18:21-35 aloud. Explain that Jesus calls us to show mercy and forgiveness in our relationships.

Say: Think of the one person in your life right now who seems most in conflict with you. Choose now to remember the debt of gratitude you owe to that person. Perhaps you'll recall past acts of kindness this person has shown you, or you'll think of when you first met. Keep thinking of ways to see this person in the best light possible until you're sure you have recognized the value of this relationship.

Give kids each a stamped postcard and a pen. Have each person write a note of appreciation to the person he or she thought about (it could even be someone in the group). Collect the cards, and remember to mail them as soon as possible.

Say: We can also show our appreciation for one another when we aren't trying to patch up arguments or conflicts. Go to three other people, and tell them something you really appreciate about them. You may say something about their personality or talents.

Close by having volunteers take turns offering one-sentence prayers, asking God to help them fight fair with friends.

Wrap-Up Option 2

Love Feast *(up to 10 minutes)*

Have kids sit in a circle. Pass a loaf of bread around, and have kids each break off a piece. Then have them each get up and offer other kids in the group a small piece of their bread. As they share one another's bread, they are to say one of two things: "My heart is peaceful when I think of you," or, "I sense conflict in our relationship. Here's what I feel…"

If there's a serious conflict, kids may need to arrange a time to talk together about it and work on a plan for resolving the conflict. After everyone has said something, have kids say one positive thing about the person on their right. For example, someone might say, "I appreciate your openness," or, "I like the things you said in class today."

Close with a circle prayer, thanking God for honest, open relationships and asking for God's help to fight fair and say, "I'm sorry."

Extra-Time Tips

Conflict Theater—Form two groups. Have one group make up and role-play a serious conflict between two preteens. Have the other group act as coaches to help the participants resolve their conflict. Have a pile-on handshake when they settle the conflict.

A Parting of Ways—Have kids read about the conflict between Paul and Barnabas in Acts 15:36-40. Form two groups, and have each group write a script for this conflict. One group will use the principles of fighting fair, and the other group will ignore those principles. Have groups present the two skits and discuss the difference conflict-resolution strategies can make in a relationship.

Fair-Fight Contract—Have kids draft a list of guidelines for fighting fairly with friends. Write the list on a poster to remain on display in your meeting room. At the bottom, write, "We pledge to fight fair and do our best to follow these guidelines." Ask willing students to sign their names to the contract.

Unfair Fighting

Photocopy and cut apart the following cards.

Foul Card 1

Scorekeeping—During a *current* argument or discussion, you bring up instances of your friend's *past* failures or wrongdoings. This keeps the focus off the problem at hand.

Loose-Lips Card A

Late again? You're *always* late! I've *never* seen you get to anything before it starts. You know, *everybody* says that about you. This is impossible!

Foul Card 2

Character-Bombing—Instead of dealing with the conflict, issue, or problem to be solved, you attack the other person's character or personality.

Loose-Lips Card B

Oh, yeah? Remember the time you borrowed my basketball and put a hole in it? And what about all those times you lost things I loaned you? Just last week you busted my bike chain. I'm not even going to mention that little incident four years ago—you know what I'm talking about…

Foul Card 3

Piling On—You think of all the "bad" things your friend *has* done, *is* doing, or *will* do, and you overwhelm him or her with it. It's like football players gang-tackling. Your friend has little chance to recover from this nonstop verbal dumping.

Loose-Lips Card C

I'm tired of you forgetting about me—like just now, making me wait for you. And yesterday you didn't call until nine o'clock. You'll probably be busy all weekend and leave me by myself, just like you forgot about my birthday. And, hey, what about your promise to help me with my math? And another thing…

Foul Card 4

Generalizing—Instead of being specific, you use words like *always*, *never*, and *every time*. You move from dealing with a particular problem to making a big deal out of *everything*.

Loose-Lips Card D

Well, all I can say is that maybe you disappointed me a little. And don't ask me to explain because I think you know what I mean. And if you don't, you should. Besides, I'm not so sure I would want a friend who couldn't understand what's upsetting me…

Foul Card 5

Fogging—You speak in such vague terms that you can't really be accused of attacking your friend. You *seem* to imply something is wrong, and your tone is rather threatening. This is the opposite of "speaking the truth in love."

Loose-Lips Card E

If only you weren't so selfish. You always want your own way. You're just about the most conceited, creepy, sleaze bag I've ever seen!

Foul Card 6

Counterattacking—Instead of really listening to a friend's complaints and responding to them, you make up your own complaints to sling right back. No communication really takes place—just a series of verbal attacks with pauses for reloading.

Loose-Lips Card F

So you think *I* ignored *you* at the party, huh? Well, I think *you* ignored *me* at the game.

Permission to photocopy this handout from Faith 4 Life™: Preteen Bible Study Series, *Handling Conflict* granted for local church use. Copyright © Group Publishing, Inc., P.O. Box 481, Loveland, CO 80539. www.grouppublishing.com

Serving God at Home

The Point: ➤ Giving and receiving trust is the key to getting along with parents.

Here's a classic statement from a preteen to a parent: "Why can't you just trust me?" Though parents *do* want to trust their kids, they're often afraid—mostly for their kids' own physical or emotional safety.

Getting together on the issue of trust will help kids and parents move toward peace in the family. Though both sides must learn to give and receive trust, it's not out of the question for kids to extend the initial invitation.

Scripture Source

1 Samuel 20:24-34

In this passage, Saul and Jonathan argue about Jonathan's friendship with David.

Saul was jealous of David, believing David's popularity among the people was a threat. He determined to eliminate the threat by killing David. But Jonathan chose to take David as a close friend and protect him from his father's schemes. Saul violently disagreed with the love and help Jonathan gave David. His reasons were quite sinful, and he was clearly in the wrong.

Preteens will see from this passage that conflict can arise when parents display sinful motives and actions. Perhaps it's typically the kids who are in the wrong—but not always. Help kids recognize that they're called to obey parents in every way that's not clearly in conflict with Christian principles for individual behavior.

Ephesians 6:1-4

In this passage, Paul describes Christian principles of behavior relating to parents and children.

The basic command is that children should obey their parents. But parents have a serious and significant responsibility too. Paul warns parents not to deliberately frustrate their children by being selfish or arbitrary in their rule-making.

Help kids recognize that peace with parents is a two-way street. Both sides have responsibilities. Preteens need to see that their primary responsibilities are respect and obedience. They need to take care of those responsibilities without trying to change their parents.

The Study at a Glance

Section	Minutes	What Students Will Do	Supplies
Warm-Up Option 1	up to 10	**A Hairy Experience**—One student arbitrarily restyles the hair of another.	Styling gel, hair spray, pick, comb, brush, Velcro curlers, squirt bottle, mirror
Warm-Up Option 2	up to 10	**At Your Command**—Designate a "boss" who gives commands to other kids.	Tape, index card, marker
Bible Connection	up to 15	**Trust or Consequences**—Kids who say they can be trusted walk around you as you hold a water balloon in your lap.	Water balloon, straight pins, extra change of clothing, towel
	up to 15	**Deadly Spears**—Identify "spears" Saul threw that destroyed Jonathan's trust and "spears" kids and parents use to damage their own relationships.	Bibles, balloons, poster board, scissors, markers, straight pins, tape
Life Application	up to 15	**Trust Check**—Evaluate trust levels and role-play techniques to raise the trust level between parents and kids.	Bible, "Trust Check" handout (p. 47), pencils
Wrap-Up Option 1	up to 5	**Holding Parents in the Light**—Form a circle of prayer.	Paper, pencils, flashlight
Wrap-Up Option 2	up to 5	**Prayer Pacts**—Partners pray for each other to successfully communicate trust-building to parents.	

Before the Study

For the "Trust or Consequences" activity, bring a change of clothes just in case kids pop the water balloon on your lap.

For the "Trust Check" activity, make a copy of the "Trust Check" handout (p. 47) for each student.

The Study

Warm-Up Option 1

A Hairy Experience *(up to 10 minutes)*

Bring a bag of hair-styling supplies to class. Include styling gel, hair spray, picks, combs, brushes, Velcro curlers, squirt bottles, and mirrors. Assign a few students to be hair stylists (make an educated guess about who the most skilled hair stylists in your class are), and assign willing volunteers to be their "stylees." Give each designated person permission to "redo" the hair of any "stylee." Have students share supplies, and encourage imagination and creativity in the new hairstyles. Explain that you'll allow up to four minutes for each makeover.

Once the makeover is complete, invite each person who did the styling to tell why he or she has created a superior hairstyle. Then hand the mirror to their "stylee" and **ask:**

- **How do you like your new look?**
- **How do you feel about having this new style forced on you? Explain.**

Then address the entire group and **ask:**

- **How is that like the way kids feel when told by their parents how to act or dress?**

Thank your "victims" for being such good sports. Allow them to wash up if desired while the class continues.

Then **say:** Sometimes in conflict situations, we try to force changes on the other person instead of working on compromise and acceptance. Parents are sometimes guilty of wanting to make their kids conform to an "ideal" image—even trying to get them to wear their hair in the "right" way!

Kids try to get their parents to change too. But forcing change almost always leads to greater conflict in the end. Today we're going to look at a new approach: giving and receiving trust. We'll learn that ▶giving and receiving trust is the key to getting along with parents.

FYI

In this study, parents are referred to often. Because many kids come from single-parent homes, be sensitive to adjust the wording to read parent *as necessary.*

FYI

If your class is larger than a dozen kids, you might want to have several makeovers going on at once. Kids who don't want to actively participate can observe and encourage the "hair stylists" and "stylees."

◀ **The Point**

FYI

If the student you choose is not assertive, take him or her aside and suggest commands to give the rest of the class, such as, "Sit up straight," "Laugh," "Don't laugh," "Keep your eyes down and don't look at anyone else," and, "Stare at the person across the table without blinking." Emphasize that none of the commands can be negative or embarrassing.

The Point ▶

Warm-Up Option 2

At Your Command (up to 10 minutes)

Find out whose birthday is closest to the present date. Tape an index card that says "The Boss" to the person's shoulder. **Say: I'm making you the boss in this classroom. For the next three minutes, we're at your command.**

At the end of three minutes, address everyone but the boss. **Ask:**

- How did you feel about being ordered around like that?
- What did you think of our boss's style of doing things?
- How was this activity like what happens at home?
- How do the feelings you had about our boss compare with the feelings you sometimes have about your parents?

Say: A big part of growing up is learning how to be your own boss. It comes little by little. Sometimes, in the middle of that process, it can be really hard to accept your parents' authority. Obedience isn't something the Bible tells us to *like*; it's something the Bible tells us to *do*. The good news is obedience leads to trust, and trust helps eliminate conflict. In this study we're going to look at trust-building and the positive effect it can have on your relationship with your parents. We'll learn that ▶ giving and receiving trust is the key to getting along with parents.

Bible Connection

Trust or Consequences (up to 15 minutes)

Sit in a chair in the middle of the room, and place a water balloon on your lap. Tell kids there's a small box of straight pins on a table at the other side of the room.

Say: Raise your hand if I can trust you to walk around me three times, with a pin in your hand, and not prick this balloon. Get kids' responses about whether they think they could do it. **Say: If you know you can't be trusted, raise your hand.**

Have the self-proclaimed trustworthy kids get straight pins and form a line, ready to march around you in a circle.

Say: OK, I'm going to close my eyes, and I want you to walk around me three times slowly, pins in hand. Then sit down again.

Be prepared for whatever transpires—bring an extra skirt or pair of pants and a towel for cleanup. Your lap may be wet, or it may still be dry when kids sit back

42 • Handling Conflict

down. There is some risk here! In either case, use these questions to debrief. **Ask:**

• **How did it feel to be trusted with something that could possibly bring pain or disappointment to an adult?**

• **How did it feel to have and keep someone's trust (or to lose someone's trust)?**

Responses will depend on whether someone pricked the water balloon. If someone did, make sure kids know this was a fun activity, that you brought a change of clothes, and no one needs to feel guilty. **Ask:**

• **How is this activity like conflicts between you and your parents?**

Say: Seriously, was there anybody here who didn't want this balloon to get popped? Who would want to miss all that fun, excitement, and humiliation? Many times, parents withhold their trust because they worry that in a tempting situation, their kids are going to go for the excitement. But ➤giving and receiving trust is the key to getting along with parents.

◄ *The Point*

Have kids follow along in their Bibles as you read aloud 1 Samuel 20:24-34. Explain the background of Saul and Jonathan's relationship from 1 Samuel chapters 18–19 and the details of the incident in 1 Samuel 20:24-34. Discuss the complicated loyalties in this conflict situation and how Jonathan managed to right a wrong and protect the innocent David without showing disrespect to his father.

Deadly Spears *(up to 15 minutes)*

Divide the class into groups of no more than six students each. Give each group a balloon to blow up and, with a marker, label it "Trust." Give each group one piece of poster board, and instruct them to cut it into long, thin spears (approximately one-inch wide)—at least one for each group member, plus several extras.

Say: Reread 1 Samuel 20:24-34, expressly looking for "spears"—breaches of trust—that Saul used to damage his relationship with his son Jonathan. Work with your group to write each of these breaches on a spear (for instance, Saul insulted or cursed at Jonathan, treated Jonathan's friend shamefully, and tried to kill Jonathan).

Then each group member should write at least one "spear" that can destroy trust between parents and their children. The "trustbuster" might be something a parent would do, something a child might do, or something they might both be guilty of.

Give teams about seven minutes to make their spears. Then distribute one straight pin for every spear. Instruct students to tape the pin to the tip of the spear so that only the smallest portion protrudes. This is a safety feature, but will still make the spears capable of easily popping the trust balloons.

Allow groups to share the spears they thought up with the rest of the class. Then count to three and allow the kids to attack and pop the trust balloons with the spears. When kids are finished, **ask:**

• **How do you think Jonathan's relationship with his father changed after this incident?**

• **Do you think Jonathan was ever able to trust his father again? Why or why not?**

• **How important is trust to our relationship with our parents?**

• **How easy is it to lose that trust and damage the relationship?**

• **How easy is it to repair the trust once it is lost?**

The Point ▶ **Say:** ▶Giving and receiving trust is the key to getting along with parents. Do everything you can to keep from being the one to damage your relationship with your parents by losing their trust. Show them that you are honest, dependable, and self-controlled.

Life Application

Trust Check *(up to 15 minutes)*

Give kids each a photocopy of the "Trust Check" handout (p. 47), a pencil, and a Bible. Have students work through the top half of the handout individually. Then have kids pair up with a partner to role-play the steps for establishing trust in a conflict area.

The Point ▶ **Say:** The Bible's approach to this issue of obedience and trust is interesting because it speaks to both parents and kids. It recognizes that ▶giving and receiving trust is the key to getting along for parents and their children. You and your partner will take turns being parents to each other. Begin by reading Ephesians 6:1-4 aloud together. Then share the conflict area you each identified on your handout. As you play the role of parents, try to identify with your partners' needs and feelings.

When students are finished, **ask:**

• **What did it feel like to play the role of a parent? What new insights did you discover?**

- **What do you think would happen if you tried this strategy in real life?**

Have kids each say something positive to the whole group about their partner's insights in this activity. For example, someone might say, "You really had a good idea about how parents see things," or, "I like the ideas you came up with."

Wrap-Up Option 1

Holding Parents in the Light *(up to 5 minutes)*

Give kids each a sheet of paper and a pencil. Have kids each draw a quick picture representing their parents or guardians. Be sensitive in your wording for kids whose parents are divorced.

Then stand in a circle, shoulder to shoulder. Turn off the lights, and hand a flashlight to the person on your left.

Say: Point the flashlight at the picture of your parent(s). Imagine that the light you're shining is the light of God's love. If there are deep feelings of hurt between you, ask God to begin to heal them now. Say a silent prayer for your relationship with your parent(s). Then pass the flashlight to the person on your left.

When the flashlight comes back to you, say "amen," and dismiss the class. Thank them for taking the time to learn how to handle conflict.

Wrap-Up Option 2

Prayer Pacts *(up to 5 minutes)*

Have kids rejoin their partners from the "Trust Check" activity. Have students each name a time this week when they'll talk about the trust-building process with their parents. Then have partners commit to pray for each other, asking for better trust and communication with parents.

Have partners close in prayer, thanking God for giving them the ability to handle conflicts in a positive way.

Extra-Time Tips

Hot List—Have kids help you develop a "hot list" of different kinds of conflicts that can happen among family members, such as wanting to watch different TV shows, waiting for the bathroom in the morning, and taking the last pancake at breakfast. Then call on volunteers to do quick Charades of one of the scenarios as the rest of the group tries to guess which one is being portrayed.

Personal Letters—Have kids write honest, open letters to their parents or guardians dealing with specific issues of trust and conflict within the home. Kids may address breaches or successes on either side—their own or their parents'. Remind students to speak the truth in love and to temper their honesty with grace and kindness.

What-if? Letters—Have kids write letters as though they were Jonathan writing to Saul about their disappointment in his actions and trying to resolve the conflict.

Parents' Panel—Invite a panel of parents to discuss and answer kids' questions from a neutral parent's perspective. If possible, find parents who don't have kids in your group.

Trust Check

Put a star in the boxes below if you have your parents' trust in these areas. Put an X in the box if this is an area of conflict between you and your parent(s). Be prepared to role-play with a partner one of those conflict areas.

- ☐ How I handle my money
- ☐ Dressing appropriately
- ☐ My choice of friends
- ☐ Getting my homework done
- ☐ Getting home when I say I will
- ☐ Being home alone
- ☐ Caring for younger brothers or sisters
- ☐ Going shopping on my own
- ☐ Being with kids of the opposite sex
- ☐ Watching TV responsibly

I'd really like to improve my parents' trust in me in this area:

Read Ephesians 6:1-4. Then role-play the steps below with a "parent" partner to improve the trust level in the area you just identified. Begin a conversation with your partner similar to the ones listed. Then have your partner respond as a parent might actually respond.

Step One: Give Trust
1. Clearly state your point of view, your needs, and your wants. Tell how your feelings relate to your requests. For example, "I'm upset that you don't let me stay out later…"

2. Listen carefully to understand the needs and wants of your parent. Find out how your parent's feelings relate to the decisions about rules and restrictions.

Step Two: Ask for Trust
1. Find out what you could do to gain your parent's trust. Ask your parent to suggest possibilities. Discuss them. Agree to start doing one of the things suggested. For example, "What can I do to build trust with you?" or, "What can I do to help you see that I'm responsible?"

2. Set a definite date and time for a follow-up conference. Talk about your performance so far.

Course Reflection

At the conclusion of the course, ask kids to form a circle. Ask students to reflect on the past four studies. Have them take turns completing the following sentences:

- **Something I learned in this course is...**
- **If I could tell my friends about this course, I'd say...**
- **Something I'll do differently because of this course is...**

To extend the learning beyond the classroom, choose one of the following ideas:

Sitcom Sit-In

Arrange a get-together outside the classroom for one or two weeks after the end of the study. Choose a night with lots of family-oriented sitcoms your students will enjoy watching. Watch the shows during a party with a couch-potato theme. (Serve potato chips, build-your-own baked potatoes, or other potato foods.) During commercial breaks, turn down the sound, and evaluate how the shows deal with conflict. Have kids answer the following questions:

- **Were the situations realistic?**
- **How did the characters cope?**
- **What should they have done differently?**
- **Were people put down or built up?**
- **What Christian dimensions of love were incorporated or left out?**
- **How would you rate the show—helpful or unhelpful?**

Conflicting Plays

Have students write and rehearse plays showing kids and adults dealing with conflict in both good and bad ways. Have students perform the plays for the whole church as part of a conflict-discussion night or just for kids' families and friends. Have a question-and-answer time after each play for participants and the audience to talk about the message in the play.